The Usborne
Little Book
of
Horses
and Ponies

The Usborne
Little Book
of
Horses
and Ponies

Sarah Khan

Designed by Kate Rimmer

Illustrated by Stephen Lambert

Digital manipulation by Keith Furnival

Consultant: Juliet Penwarden, BHS II

Edited by Kirsteen Rogers

Usborne Quicklinks

The Usborne Quicklinks Website is packed with thousands of links to all the best websites on the internet. The websites include information, video clips, sounds, games and animations that support and enhance the information in Usborne internet-linked books.

To visit the recommended websites for the *Little Book of Horses and Ponies*, go to the Usborne Quicklinks Website at **www.usborne-quicklinks.com** and enter the keywords: **little horses**

Internet safety

When using the internet please follow the internet safety guidelines displayed on the Usborne Quicklinks Website. The websites recommended at Usborne Quicklinks are regularly reviewed. However, the content of a website may change at any time and Usborne Publishing is not responsible for the content of websites other than its own. We recommend that children are supervised while on the internet.

Contents

6   About horses

8   Types of horse

10 Shades and patches

12 Growing up

14 Horse behaviour

16 Making friends

18 On the move

20 Breaking in

22 Riding styles

24 Dressage

26 Show jumping

28 Gymkhanas

30 Horse trials

32 At the races

34 More horse sports

36 Horse shows

38 Performing horses

40 At the rodeo

42 Riding out

44 At the stables

46 Food and feeding

48 Grooming

50 Shoeing

52 Staying healthy

54 Clothing

56 Horse power

58 Horses at work

60 How to draw horses

62 Amazing but true

64 Index

Horses' earliest ancestors were small, woodland creatures.

About horses

Horses and ponies have been an important part of people's lives for thousands of years. Today, these faithful companions and tireless workers frolic in fields, gallop around racecourses, and labour on farms all over the world.

Early ancestors

The first horses were small, deer-like creatures that lived around 50 million years ago. Very slowly, they developed into animals that look more like the horses you see today.

The taming of the horse

For thousands of years, people hunted wild horses for food. Then, around 5,000 years ago, they began to keep them in herds, and bred them for their milk, skins and meat. Later, people realized they could train horses for riding, and pulling vehicles.

The ancestors of these mustang horses were tamed and bred in Spain, then taken to America to help Spanish settlers explore their new country.

The main points

The different parts of a horse's body are called its points. Here are the points mentioned in this book.

The height of a horse or pony is measured from the ground to the top of its withers, in units called hands. A hand is equivalent to 10cm (4in).

Forelock
Poll
Mane
Withers
Back
Flank
Hindquarters
Tail
Muzzle
Knee
Elbow
Cannon bone
Hoof
Hock
Fetlock

Horse or pony?

Whether an animal is called a horse or a pony depends mainly on its body shape. In general, ponies are smaller, with stockier legs and shorter, plumper bodies. An animal's height can give you a quick clue, too. If it's taller than 59 inches – which, in horse terms, is expressed as 14 hands and 3 inches, or 14.3 hands – it's likely to be a horse.

Shetland ponies are one of the smallest pony breeds, but they are also very strong.

Here are some places where you might see purebred horses and ponies...

U Riding stables

U Racing stables or racecourses

U Horse shows

U Stud farms, where horses are bred

U The breed's natural surroundings, such as British moors, French lowlands, or Austrian mountains

Types of horse

Worldwide, there are over 300 breeds of horse and pony. Most animals are crossbred, which means they are descended from different breeds. Those whose ancestors have been of the same type for generations are described as purebred.

Breed features

At first, it can be tricky to tell what type of horse or pony you're looking at, but if you search for certain features, you can pick up clues to an animal's breed.

Arab horse — Dished profile

Horses and ponies with **Arab** blood usually have a curved-in face – called a dished profile – and hold their tails high.

Thoroughbred

Thoroughbreds are tall, long-legged horses with a light build and fine coat.

Draught horses are big, slow animals with broad features, and long hairs – called feather – around their feet.

Mountain and moorland ponies are small and sturdy with a long, rough coat.

8

Welsh mountain ponies like this one are hardy and sure-footed, and cope well with bad weather and rough ground.

One of the oldest breeds of horse is the Mongolian Przewalski. These rare animals have never been tamed and live in forests and on grasslands in Mongolia, and in zoos all over the world.

Before the invention of tractors, Shirehorses were commonly used as draught horses to pull ploughs across fields.

Job descriptions

Horses can be described by the kinds of job they are suited to. Lightweight breeds used mainly for riding, such as Andalusians, are called riding horses. Harness horses, such as Hackneys, are heavier and can pull light vehicles. Draught horses, such as Shirehorses are the bulkiest, so can pull heavy vehicles.

Mixing it up

On rare occasions, horses and ponies breed with similar animals, such as donkeys and zebras. Their young – described as hybrids – can be used as work horses or kept as pets.

Hybrid names

Mule
male donkey + female horse

Hinny
female donkey + male horse

Zebroid
any zebra + any horse

Zebra hinny
female zebra + male donkey

Shades and patches

Even if they're the same breed, no two horses look exactly alike. The colour of their coat and their pattern and patches give each one its own individual look.

When they are first born, Camargue ponies have black or brown coats, but turn grey as they grow into adults.

Grey

Hair colours

Horses and ponies are described according to the shade and pattern of their coats, manes and tails. Here are some of the main colours you might come across.

Bays have black manes and tails, and their lower legs can be black, too. Their coats range in shade from blackish brown to gold.

Chestnut

Chestnut horses have reddish-brown hair. Their manes and tails may be a shade lighter or darker than their bodies.

Grey coats can be any shade from white to dark grey. They contain a mixture of black and white hairs growing from dark skin.

Yellow dun

Yellow dun horses have a yellow or orangey-brown coat and often have a dark stripe running down the length of their backs.

Roans have an even mixture of coloured and white hairs. **Strawberry roans** have chestnut and white; **blue roans** have black and white.

White coats with patches of colour are called **piebald** if the patches are black, and **skewbald** if they are any other colour.

This young piebald horse has a white coat with black patches.

White bits

Horses and ponies often have patches of white hair on their heads or legs. These markings have different names, depending on their shape and size.

A white patch on a horse's forehead, like this, is called a star.

A stocking is a white patch on a horse's leg that stretches up from its hoof to its knee, or higher.

There are different names for horses as they grow from babies to adults.

U **Foal**
a male or female up to one year old

U **Yearling**
a male or female between one and two years old

U **Filly**
a female between one and four years old

U **Colt**
a male between one and four years old

U **Mare**
a female over four years old

U **Stallion**
a male over four years old

Growing up

Baby horses and ponies are called foals, and most are born in spring. In its first days, a foal only drinks its mother's milk, but it starts to eat solids after a couple of weeks. Food, exercise and attention from its mother are everything a little foal needs to grow healthy and strong.

A foal's features

Foals have soft, fuzzy coats and long chin-whiskers. Those that are born in winter have woolly, extra-thick coats to keep them warm. Newborns have short, fluffy tails that become longer and rougher as they grow.

At just a week old, this foal has spent most of its time resting, but will soon become more active.

Familiar scents

A newborn foal starts learning about the world through its sense of smell. Mothers and foals touch noses so they can recognize each other by their scents.

Getting stronger

Only half an hour after being born, a foal can stand on its feet and, after just a few hours, it can walk and even run. Each day it grows a little sturdier, as its body strengthens from the feet up. First its hooves get harder and its legs get thicker, then the rest of its body grows.

A newborn foal is wobbly on its feet at first but quickly learns to steady itself.

This foal's legs are nearly as long as its mother's. This helps it to keep up when it gallops alongside her.

Growth spurt

When it's first born, a foal is about the same height as its mother's belly. It continues to grow until it is at least three years old, but some horses and ponies can still be growing right up to the age of five.

A foal is usually 60% of its adult height at birth and 95% of its adult height by the time it's 18 months old.

Horse behaviour

How horses behave and communicate is based on instincts they have developed over thousands of years to help them survive in the wild. But while horses are sensitive, they also enjoy the company of other animals, including people.

Like most herds, this one is led by a dominant male stallion.

Ears tipped forward

Chomping movements with mouth

Foals show older horses in their herd respect by greeting them with facial movements.

The leader of the pack

Horses can feel lonely and unsettled on their own because, in the wild, they live in herds. To stop horses within a herd fighting one another, each one has a rank or position. Dominant horses lead the way, and eat and drink first; submissive ones follow and show respect. When a person rides a horse, they are taking the place of the herd leader and the horse obeys them.

Body language

You can tell a lot about a horse's mood by the way it holds itself and moves different parts of its body. Horses use body language to give each other very clear messages.

When a horse is feeling angry or upset, it lays its ears back and swishes its tail. If it is afraid, it tucks its tail between its legs.

If a horse is excited or interested in something, it holds its tail high, pricks its ears forward and arches its neck.

A relaxed horse may flick its ears around and rest a hind leg by taking the weight off it.

Angry and upset horse

Excited or interested horse

Making sounds

Horses make a huge variety of sounds to communicate. They neigh and whinny to contact each other or people, blow through their nostrils when meeting each other for the first time, and give a soft neigh, called a nicker, as a friendly "hello".

This horse is giving a loud yawn as a way of showing its owner that it's sleepy.

Making friends

Some horses and ponies are used to being around people, while others are nervous in the company of humans, especially strangers. Whether an animal is confident or jittery, it's best to go carefully and slowly when you approach it for the first time.

If you look straight into a horse's eyes as you approach, it might feel threatened. In the wild, only its predators would look directly into its eyes.

If you're approaching a horse in a stall, call or talk to it softly to let it know you're there.

A sideways approach

A horse has eyes on each side of its head, so it can see nearly all the way around. But the position of its eyes also means that it can't see directly behind or in front. Because of this, it's best to approach a horse from the side so as not to startle it.

Trusted scent

Horses recognize each other and the people around them by smell. When you walk up to a horse, stretch out your arms, then allow it to smell the back of your hand. This way, it will know that you are a friend and it can trust you.

If a horse blows warm air onto your hand, it's a sign that it wants to be friends.

Have a chat

If you talk to a horse, it won't understand exactly what you're saying but it will be able to interpret your tone of voice. Speak gently in an even tone so that you don't make the horse nervous. If you know the horse's name, use it as often as possible as this is something it's likely to recognize.

Keep in touch

In the wild, horses scratch and stroke each other to show affection, and you can copy this gentle stroking. But some parts of a horse's body, such as its muzzle and belly, are very sensitive, so it's best to avoid touching these areas at first.

A horse reacts up to four times faster than a person to things that frighten it, so it can kick out very suddenly if it is startled.

This girl is introducing herself in a calm, gentle way, setting the horse at ease.

A horse will find it soothing if you stroke and pat it around its forehead and neck, like this.

On the move

The different ways a horse or pony moves at various speeds are called gaits or paces. You can tell which gait a horse is using by looking at its speed, watching how its legs move and counting along with the rhythm its hooves beat out as it goes along.

Walking

A walking horse moves each leg in turn, so its hooves beat out a four-time rhythm (you can count "one, two, three, four"). First, it brings forward the left back leg, then the left front leg, the right back leg and finally the right front leg.

Trotting

Trotting, or jogging, has a two-time beat, because a trotting horse's legs move in pairs. Trotting can feel bumpy for a rider, but it looks smooth.

When a horse is relaxed, it might flap its ears up and down in time with its hooves as it moves.

Horses nod their heads slightly as they walk.

As this foal trots, it brings its back leg and opposite front leg forward together.

Cantering

A canter, also called a lope, is faster and smoother than a trot, and has a three-time gait. When cantering, a horse brings either of its back legs forward first, followed by two diagonally opposite legs at the same time, then the remaining leg.

A canter is a lively, bounding pace.

Galloping

A gallop is faster than a canter and it has a four-time beat, because the horse's legs land separately. It can be hard to control a galloping horse, so only experienced riders try it.

A gallop is a horse's fastest pace. This galloping horse can reach a speed of about 65kph (40mph).

Halt

In a square halt, a horse stands straight and still with its weight spread evenly over its four legs. Both front and back legs are placed opposite each other.

A flying pace is a smooth, fast gait that only Icelandic horses can do. It involves moving two legs on the same side forward together.

Breaking in

If a horse is handled gently in the first years of its life, it becomes used to people and will be ready to accept a rider by the time it's three or four years old. Training a horse to be ridden is called breaking it in.

Getting started

The first thing a young horse needs to get used to is the feel of a saddle on its back. The trainer first puts a large pad, called a numnah, on the horse's back, then puts the saddle on top.

Before it can be ridden, a horse needs a mouthpiece, called a bit. Long leather straps, called reins, are attached to the bit, and the trainer uses these to control the horse. First, the trainer lets the horse smell the bit, then slowly places it in the horse's mouth, letting it get used to the new feeling.

A bit is attached to straps which go around a horse's muzzle and head. This headgear is called a bridle.

Going around in circles

To teach a horse how to respond to voice commands, a trainer puts it on a long rein called a lunge or longe. While the trainer holds one end of the rein, the horse circles around, learning to stop and start at its trainer's request. Lungeing also helps the horse to improve its balance and gaits without a rider's weight on its back.

Trainers use lungeing to teach horses to respond to commands such as "walk on", "trot on", "canter" and "whoa".

Lunge ropes are usually made of strong but soft cotton or nylon, so they don't break easily but are comfortable to hold.

Taking a seat

Once a horse is used to wearing a saddle, its trainer can start getting it used to being ridden. The trainer starts by leaning over the horse's back as it's standing still and, over several sessions, gradually progresses to sitting in the saddle.

After a few days of training sessions, this horse has become comfortable enough to move around with a rider sitting in its saddle.

Riding styles

There are two main styles of riding: classical and Western. These developed in different parts of the world, so the way people ride often depends on where they're from. It also depends on what the rider wants to do; each style suits some activities better than others.

A classical rider, with the reins in both hands

A classical history

Classical riding developed in Europe. Originally, horses were used in times of war, and trained to be swift and brave on chaotic battlefields. This led to a style in which horses could perform precise and difficult movements at their rider's command.

Classical riders use balance rather than grip to stay secure, and they hold the horse's reins in both hands. To help them balance, they sit in the classical riding position, with their shoulders, hips and heels lined up. Their feet are supported by hoops called stirrups, which hang down from the saddle.

Into the West

Western riding developed in America and is based on the way early Spanish settlers in America rode their horses when rounding up herds of cattle. In the 1770s, the first cowboys spent a lot of time on horseback. They adopted the Spanish style because it was comfortable, and left one hand free to rope cattle.

A Western rider, with the reins in one hand, so one arm is free

In the Western style, riders hold their horses' reins in just one hand and sit upright. They use their legs to grip onto the horse, and have long stirrups.

Using the styles

Many people ride in the classical style simply for pleasure, but it is also used for many competitive activities such as show jumping, gymkhanas and cross-country.

The Western riding style is ideal for riding over long distances and trail riding. It is also the style used in rodeos, mounted games and parades.

Western parades take place all over America and Canada.

Dressage

Dressage is a complicated form of classical riding. In dressage competitions (which are also called tests) a horse performs different movements to show off how graceful it is and demonstrate how well the horse and rider work together.

Dressage tests are divided into levels that range in difficulty from preliminary up to advanced. The higher the level, the more complex the movements.

This dressage rider is making slight movements to give the horse precise instructions on how and where to move.

Moving on

The most basic part of a dressage test is to show how well a horse can move at a walk, trot and canter, and how smoothly it can change from one pace to another.

Competition judges also look for horses that can vary the length of their steps at each pace without changing their speed. The horses need to stay balanced and in rhythm while they go in straight lines, change direction, and move in circles.

On the spot

At the advanced levels of dressage, horses learn how to raise and lower their legs without moving forwards. They trot on the spot, raising their legs very high, and also trot very slowly, making it seem as if they're floating above the ground in slow motion.

Points and penalties

In a test, each movement performed by a horse is given a score out of ten by a judge or panel of judges. The judges give low marks for faults, such as loss of rhythm, loss of balance, stiff movements, moving in a crooked line, and ignoring the rider's commands.

A pirouette is a difficult movement. The horse pivots around, moving its front legs in a circle around its back legs.

The rider should stay balanced.

The horse should be calm.

The horse should move gracefully, following the rider's every instruction.

This is how a judge marks a horse's performance of a dressage movement:

10 excellent
9 very good
8 good
7 quite good
6 satisfactory
5 sufficient (good enough)
4 insufficient (not good enough)
3 quite bad
2 bad
1 very bad
0 did not perform

Show jumping

In show jumping competitions, entrants have to ride their horses over a course made up of a series of fences and walls, called jumps. Most competitions have two rounds.

There are different categories in a show jumping competition. Classes are usually divided according to the age, experience or height of the horse.

Fences, walls and bars

Show jumps are obstacles that fall down easily if a horse knocks them. There are two basic types: uprights, which are tall and thin, and spreads, which are lower but wide. Within these categories, there are a variety of jumps. Here are some of the ones you see most often:

An **upright rail fence** is a vertical jump, with several poles set above one another.

A **wall** is an upright made out of wooden blocks and one or more pale top stones.

A **staircase fence** or **triple bar** is a spread with three rails at ascending heights.

Parallel bars form a spread fence with two horizontal poles at the same height.

A **water jump** is a water-filled ditch, often with a fence in front of it.

An upright rail fence

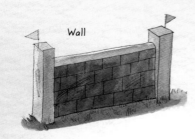

Wall

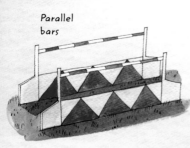

Parallel bars

26

Faults and penalties

Judges give the competitors penalty points
for any faults they make, such as going over
the time limit, running beside a jump instead
of jumping over it, knocking a jump down,
or refusing to go over it. Competitors
with the fewest penalties compete
again. In this second round, if the
two best riders have the same
number of penalties, the winner
is the one who finished the
course the quickest.

If a horse repeatedly refuses to
jump, the competitor is knocked
out of the competition.

Tackling a spread fence, the
challenge for this horse is
to jump over a width as
well as a height.

This girl is running alongside her pony as part of a gymkhana game.

Gymkhanas

Gymkhanas are riding competitions which involve different races, or mounted games. The games often look simple, but each one is designed to test the rider's and the horse's skill, athleticism and training. Games and their rules vary between competitions.

Speed games

Competitors in a speed game have to get from one end of the gymkhana arena to the other and back again as quickly as they can, overcoming obstacles along the way.

A **stepping stone dash** involves the competitors riding to a row of stepping stones, dismounting and running along them. They then jump back onto their horses and ride to the finish.

In a **sack race**, the competitors ride to the middle of the arena, dismount and get into sacks. Then, they shuffle and jump along, leading their horses to the finish line.

Precision games

Precision games need more than just speed; they test skills such as balance and hand-eye coordination, too.

During a **flag race**, riders have to take a flag from one container and put it into another at high speed, without dismounting.

As the container fills up, it becomes harder to fit in more flags.

In a **ball and bucket game**, riders collect balls and drop them into a bucket. When all the balls are in the bucket, the competitors race to the finish.

There are several types of **mug races**. One involves riders collecting mugs and placing them on top of a row of bending poles.

Team games

Team games are often races with change-overs, where equipment is handed from one team member to the next. One of these is **postman's chase**. A rider collects a letter to put in a sack they are carrying. Then they pass the sack to the next team member, who rides off to collect the next letter.

In many team games, each member has to ride in and out of a line of poles to reach the other end of the arena.

Horse trials

Horse trials – also called events – combine
at least three different disciplines in one
competition. The main three are dressage,
show jumping and cross-country. Trials can
take place over one, two or three days.

Dressage event

The dressage event is usually held first in a
trial. During this event, riders have to show
that their horses can perform an exact
sequence of movements with balance, rhythm
and suppleness, obeying their every command.

Dressage riders have to be
smartly turned out.

Show jumping event

Show jumping often
follows dressage
in a horse
trial.

In the show jumping phase of a horse
trial, the horses have to jump over
a series of fences. The number of
fences ranges from 10 to 14. These
obstacles are generally easy
to jump, but the course has
twists and turns which
test the horse's fitness,
agility and obedience.

Cross-country event

In the cross-country event, competitors tackle a course made up of anything from 20 to 32 jumps. The jumps are difficult and varied. These are just a few of the obstacles a competitor might have to overcome:

Log pile – a wide stack of logs

Chair – a wide, wooden obstacle in the shape of a bench

Bale frame – a row of hay bales

Step fence – forms the shape of steps going down a hillside

Other events

Long horse trials also include speed and endurance tests, where entrants compete in steeplechases, and road and track races. During a steeplechase, horses have to clear a course of 10 or 12 fences and ditches in a fixed time. If they go over that time, they are given penalty points.

At the start of longer trials, the horses are checked by a vet. They're inspected again after the cross-country phase to see if they are still fit enough to go on to other events.

This horse has just ridden through a pool of water in a cross-country event.

At the races

Horse racing is one of the oldest sports in the world. The most popular types of races are flat races with no obstacles, and steeplechases where the horses jump fences at speed.

Horse racing was one of the events in the Olympic Games in ancient Greece over 2,500 years ago. The races were dangerous, because the ground was rough and uneven, and the riders had no stirrups or saddles.

Race preparation

Horses arrive early at a racecourse so they can get used to their new surroundings. They are led into stables where they are guarded strictly; only the people who work with the horses are allowed to visit them.

Horses travel to racecourses in trailers or trucks called horseboxes.

Parading around

From the stables, the horses are taken to a parade ring beside the racecourse. This gives the people who've come to watch the race a chance to see the horses walking around and to decide which one they think will win. The jockeys then mount their horses, and helpers lead them to the racecourse.

Walking around a parade ring gives a horse the chance to stretch its legs before the race.

32

And they're off

At the start of a flat racecourse, there is a row of compartments called starting stalls, with one stall for each horse. A person called a "starter" climbs onto a platform beside the course and raises a flag. Then the starter lowers the flag, presses a button to open the front of the stalls, and the race begins.

A horse that quickly pulls out in front of the others and stays in the leading position, like this, is called a front-runner.

A close finish

When a few horses finish at almost the same time, it's the job of a judge beside the finish line to decide which horse has won. If it's too close for judges to decide, they will look at footage taken by cameras on both sides of the finish line.

The winners

Immediately after the race, the horses that have come first, second and third are taken to a part of the ground called a winners' enclosure. There, the owner and trainer of the winning horse, and the jockey who rode it, are presented with a prize.

The winning jockey may be presented with a trophy and receive a cash prize.

More horse sports

All around the world, people from different cultures and countries take part in a variety of horse races and games on horseback.

The carts used in harness racing are light, weighing around 18kg (40lbs).

Harness racing

Popular in the USA, harness racing, also called trotting racing, involves horses pulling their rider in small, two-wheeled carts called sulkies. The racecourse is usually 1 mile (about 1.5km) long. In some races, horses trot around the course; in others, they use a jolting, bumpy gait called a pace, which is a little faster and involves the horse bringing two legs on the same side forward together.

Hurdles are the lowest type of racing fence, so hurdling is the fastest of the jumping races.

Hurdling

In a hurdle race, horses have to clear at least eight jumps, called hurdles. A hurdle is made from bars of wood and leafy twigs, and is set in the ground at an angle. In Ireland, hurdling is more popular than flat racing.

Polo

Polo was invented in Iran over 2,500 years ago. It's a team sport played on horseback. There are four people in each team and the aim of the game is to score goals against the other side. Players score by driving a small plastic or wooden ball into the other team's goal by hitting it with a long-handled stick, called a mallet.

Horseball

First played in France in the 1970s, horseball is like netball on horseback. Players throw a ball to each other, and score goals by shooting it into a metal hoop at each end of the pitch. The ball has six leather handles attached to it, making it easier to grip.

Polo is played at a gallop and is the fastest team game in the world.

After catching the ball, a player isn't allowed to hold onto it for more than ten seconds.

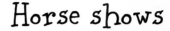

Horse shows

In a showing competition, judges assess horses and ponies on how they look, behave and move. A horse show is made up of separate competitions for horses of different type, breed, size and age.

In some horse shows, as many as 12 prizes are given in each competition. The prizes can be rosettes, medals, trophies or money.

Putting on a show

When the horses are shown to the judges, their owners ride or lead them around a judging ring while the judges watch from the middle. After moving around in a group, the horses are lined up so that each one can do an individual display, showing how it performs at different gaits. Then it stands still, so that the judges can inspect it at close range.

Judges make notes on each horse's movements, behaviour and appearance.

The winning formula

As well as grace, beauty and health, judges look for horses that have good manners. A show horse must be calm and obedient, but also confident and eager. Judges like to see horses that are friendly and enjoy being shown.

Brush-in patterns

Some competitors brush patterns into a horse's hindquarters and flanks to decorate and show off its body. These are made by brushing the horse's hair at different angles to create patches of light and dark on the horse's coat. The patterns only show up on a coat that is shiny and clean.

Shapes, such as squares, diamonds and zigzags can be brushed in freehand or using a stencil.

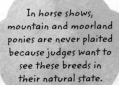

Plaits

Show horses often have plaited manes to make them look smarter. Also, judges look at the shape of a horse's head and neck, and having a plaited mane helps to show off these features clearly. The style of the plait affects the way the neck looks.

In horse shows, mountain and moorland ponies are never plaited because judges want to see these breeds in their natural state.

A row of little plaits, like this, can make a horse's neck look longer. Fewer, thicker plaits can make a neck seem shorter.

Plaits laid flat down the side of the neck make it look narrower.

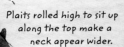

Plaits rolled high to sit up along the top make a neck appear wider.

37

Performing horses

Horses have been entertaining audiences since ancient Roman times. Today, they continue to show their skill, grace and beauty, performing in arenas and on film sets all over the world.

Vaulting

Vaulting is a sport where the participants perform gymnastic moves on the back of a cantering horse. In the past, Ancient Romans and knights in Medieval Europe learned vaulting as part of their basic riding training. These days, there are vaulting competitions in which teams perform exercises and are given scores based on form, grace and precision.

Circus acts

Animals aren't used in circuses as much as they once were, but some circuses still feature performing horses, known as rosinbacks. These horses canter around the ring while riders stand on their back and perform balancing acts.

A performing horse that was famous in Elizabethan times, is mentioned in Shakespeare's play "Love's Labours Lost". The horse, called Morocco, could dance, and "count" by stamping its foot.

Vaulters perform complicated routines, such as going from a seated position to a handstand, on the back of a moving horse.

Dancing shows

In the Austrian capital city, Vienna, an institute called the Spanish Riding School trains horses to perform complex classical riding movements in time to music. The horses are all Lipizzaners, a grey-coated Austrian breed. People come from all over the world to watch the Lipizzaners perform their spectacular shows in the Grand Hall of the school, which was once a royal ballroom.

This Lipizzaner has been trained to perform "airs above ground", which is a series of complex leaps and rises.

Stunt horses

The horses you see in films or on television are often highly trained. Many have to perform particular actions at specific times during filming, just like human actors. Horses also work with stunt riders, who perform dangerous feats such as hanging off them by a strap or jumping on and off when a horse is running at a gallop.

Stunt horses have to stay calm and focused in the most dangerous action scenes.

Roughstock riders show that
they're only holding on with
one hand by raising their free
hand in the air.

At the rodeo

Rodeos began around a hundred years ago
in the American West. Cowboys would meet
up and take turns to show how well they
could rope cattle or stay on an untamed
horse. Modern rodeos are a series of events
held in front of large audiences, in which the
contestants compete for big prizes.

Roughstock events

The three wildest, most dangerous events
in a rodeo are called roughstock events. In
all three, the rider has to stay on a bucking
animal, using only one hand to ride.

Saddle bronc riding involves a rider
having to stay seated on an untamed horse
for at least eight seconds.

Bareback bronc riding is like
saddle bronc riding, only the
competitor isn't allowed to
use a saddle, reins or stirrups.

Bull riding is like bareback
bronc riding, but the rider is
on a bull instead of a horse.

Timed events

In another series of challenges, called timed events, it's speed that counts. Judges record the time for each task and the rider that completes it in the quickest time wins.

In **steer wrestling**, the rider tries to catch a young bull (the steer). When the rider draws level with the steer's head, he leans over and tries to wrestle it down onto its side.

Barrel racing is a women's event. The riders race in a cloverleaf pattern, between and around three large oil drums.

In a barrel race, the riders have to get as close as they can to the barrels without knocking them over.

In **tie-down roping**, the rider lassos a calf's head, jumps off the horse, then ties up the calf's legs.

Team roping is the only team event. Two riders try to catch a bull by throwing lassos around its head and legs.

Some rodeos include chuckwagon races. Horses pull canvas-covered wagons, like ones that were used as mobile kitchens by people travelling across America in the 1800s.

Here are a few ways to stay safe when riding outdoors.

U Keep a distance of about the length of two horses between your horse and the one in front.

U Stay with the group, keeping at the speed of the least experienced of the riders.

U Warn riders behind you of low branches, stumps, holes or other hazards.

U Go up and down steep hills at a walking pace.

Riding out

Riding out – in the countryside, and on beaches and roads – can be exciting, but also unpredictable. The weather and the condition of the ground can change, and there are hazards, such as traffic, natural obstacles and fences to deal with. It's best for inexperienced riders to ride out with an organized group.

Treks and trails

Trekking and trail riding involves riding in groups, rambling at a slow pace off the beaten track through the countryside or along beaches. These are long trips that are often organized by riding schools or pony clubs, and are usually suitable for beginners. On treks, people ride in the classical style; on trails, they ride in the Western style.

Trekking can be ideal for a group like this one, which is made up of riders of different ages and levels of experience.

Hacks

Hacking is only suitable for experienced riders. On a hack, small groups of riders explore the countryside, walking along roads and tracks, and trotting or cantering over open ground where it is safe to do so.

After an energetic hack, these horses are walking to cool down before returning to the stables.

Drag hunts

Hunting on horseback began in the Middle Ages. These days, one of the most popular types of hunting is drag hunting, in which riders try to catch up with a person running over open countryside. The runner is given a long head start before the riders begin the chase. They follow a pack of hounds, which are tracking the smell of a strongly scented rag carried by the runner. The rag can be scented with aniseed, paraffin or animal dung. Once "caught", the runner rewards the dogs with biscuits.

Drag hunting horses need to be sure-footed, because they have to gallop and jump on uneven ground.

At the stables

Most horses can live outside all year round, but some owners keep their animals in stables for warmth and safety. Stabled horses need a lot of care because they can't look after themselves as they would do outdoors.

It's good if a stable has a half-door, like this, so the horse can look out.

On the inside

The best stables are simple, with just a few fixtures and fittings. There should be a metal ring on the wall to tie the horse to, a light high up on the ceiling, a plastic tub for the horse's food, and a fire extinguisher close by.

These are the features of a good stable:

∪ It's at least 4x4m (13x13ft).

∪ It's built of brick or wood.

∪ The bottom half of the inside walls is covered by wooden boards.

∪ The doorway is around 2m (7ft) wide and 2¹/₂m (8ft) tall.

A horse's feeding tub is called a manger.

Bedding down

Horses need a deep, clean and comfortable bed to sleep on. Their bedding can be made of straw, wood shavings or shredded newspaper, and is spread out in a thick layer over the stable floor. You'll often see the bedding built up higher around the walls of a stable to keep out draughts.

Bedding straw is usually made of wheat stalks, because a horse would eat any other kind of straw.

Mucking out

A horse can produce 13-22kg (30-50lbs) of dung every day, so its stable needs to be mucked out daily. This means clearing out the manure – the horse's dung and dirty bedding – and sweeping the stable floor.

It's best to muck out in old clothes and rubber boots.

New straw

How to muck out

1. To keep the horse out of the way, let it out into its field or tie it up outside the stable.

2. Use a pitchfork to lift the manure into a wheelbarrow. Stack any clean bedding into a corner of the stable.

3. Sweep the floor. Take the manure to a muck heap, leaving any wet patches in the stable to dry off.

4. Spread out the clean bedding with a pitchfork, and add new bedding on top.

These are some of the
grasses and herbs that
are good for horses:

∪ Rye grass

∪ Meadow fescue

∪ Timothy

∪ Crested dogstail

∪ Cocksfoot

∪ White clover

Food and feeding

Horses and ponies have small stomachs designed to cope with a little food at a time. Their natural food is grass and, in the wild, they wander around, grazing on grass for about 16 hours a day. A horse that is kept in a field can survive on grass alone during the summer, but needs extra food during the winter. If it lives in a stable, it needs to be fed at least three times every day.

Good and bad grazing

Fields where horses graze are called paddocks. The best ones have a mixture of grasses and herbs. But, before letting their animal graze, horse owners have to pull out poisonous plants from the paddock and its surrounding area. Foxgloves, ragwort, bracken, horsetail and deadly nightshade are all dangerous for horses.

This horse is slowly chewing on a prickly thistle. The plant won't harm the horse if it eats it carefully.

←--˗'

Eating out

Through winter, horses that live in paddocks are given dried grass, called hay. At any time of year, if a horse is being ridden regularly, it need buckets of extra, high-energy food too, such as grains, sugar beet or horse cubes, which are small pellets of dried food.

A feeding bucket shouldn't have handles if it is to be set on the ground, like this. The horse's leg could get caught in a handle.

A stable diet

A horse that is kept in a stable needs hay all year round so that it can eat whenever it wants to. If it's being ridden a lot, it needs high-energy food as well, just like an outdoor horse. Some stabled horses don't get to eat any fresh grass, so need other fresh foods, such as apples and carrots.

If you feed a horse with your hand, hold your palm out flat.

47

Grooming

In the wild, a horse's coat naturally suits its needs and the season of the year. But a horse that's ridden, and especially one that lives in a stable, needs extra help to keep its coat in tip-top condition. Brushing and cleaning an animal's body is called grooming. Being groomed not only cleans the horse, but also helps the blood under its skin to flow well, and keeps its coat smooth and glossy.

Grooming outdoor horses

Horses that live outside often groom themselves. If they feel itchy or sweaty, they roll on the ground or rub themselves against trees. You might spot two horses with their necks intertwined, grooming each other with their teeth.

As this horse grooms its foal, it's not only cleaning it, but bonding with it, too.

A horse that is kept in a paddock only needs its rider to groom it lightly. A full groom would remove oils from its coat that keep it waterproof and warm.

A full groom

If a horse is in a stable, it needs to be groomed thoroughly every day, as it won't have the space to groom itself. During a full groom, a horse's body, face, feet, mane and tail are cleaned using a variety of different brushes, combs, cloths and scrapers. This grooming equipment includes:

Grooming equipment can only do its job if it's kept clean. Here's how horse brushes can be kept in good condition.

U Comb out dirt and hair with a metal comb.

U Suck out dust and bits of dirt with a vacuum.

U Soak the brushes in a bucket of lukewarm soapy water.

A dandy brush, with long, stiff bristles for brushing off mud

A body brush, with short soft bristles for removing grease and dirt

Different sponges for wiping the eyes, lips and nostrils, and bottom

A stable rubber for drying and polishing the coat

A rubber curry comb for brushing off loose hair

A water brush for damping down the mane and tail

Always stand to the side of the horse to avoid being kicked.

A hoofpick for cleaning dirt and stones out of the feet

Shoeing

When a horse is ridden, its feet support the rider's weight as well as its own. This means they have to deal with a lot of wear and tear, so tame horses and ponies are fitted with metal shoes to protect the walls of their hooves. The shoes are fitted by a farrier.

Shoe selection

The type of shoe a horse wears depends on the kinds of work it does. Horses that are used for general riding, for example, have tough, iron "hunter shoes", which give a good grip on soft ground. Racehorses are usually fitted with shoes called racing plates. These are made of lightweight aluminium and help the horses run quickly.

Here's how you can tell that a horse's shoe needs replacing:

U The shoe has come off.

U The shoe is worn down.

U The nails that hold the shoe on have risen up at the ends.

U The shoe is loose – you can hear it clank on the road or a hard surface.

All types of horseshoes need daily cleaning to remove any dirt or small stones lodged underneath.

Racing plates have a shallow groove.

A hunter shoe's groove is deeper.

Wearing down

A horse's hooves are always growing. In the wild, horses' feet wear down naturally as they roam. But, with shoes on, a horse's feet don't wear down in this way and need to be trimmed. If they aren't, the horse can become lame. Horses need a farrier every six weeks or so to trim their hooves and replace their shoes.

Farriers have to be very precise when trimming hooves. If just one hoof is left ragged, too long, or too short, the horse will be unbalanced.

The farrier's tools don't hurt the horse — horses can't feel anything in the outer wall of their hooves.

A good fit

Before fitting a horseshoe, a farrier cleans out the horse's hoof, clips off any extra growth, then smooths and levels off the surface. Only then can the shoe be nailed onto the hoof. Most shoes are specially made to fit the horse's foot and are adjusted as they are being fitted. As a finishing touch, the farrier smooths off the shoe and hoof, getting rid of any sharp edges.

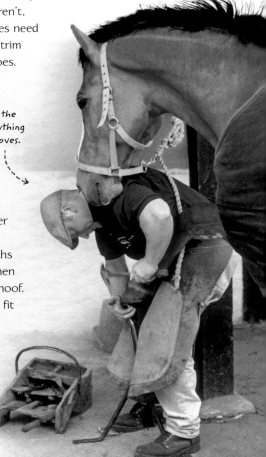

Staying healthy

There are lots of ways to ensure that a horse or pony is healthy and happy, but even the most well looked-after animal can develop an illness. Fortunately, most health problems can be treated if they're spotted early enough.

Every minute, a healthy, resting horse should be taking between eight and twelve regular breaths, and its heart should beat between 36 and 42 times.

Preventing illness

Here are some common horse diseases that are easy to prevent.

Flu and **tetanus** can be prevented with a course of injections.

Worms can be avoided by giving a horse worming powder every six weeks.

Dental disease can be kept at bay by visits from a horse dentist or vet every six months.

Horse dentists check for swellings on the face — a sign of gum disease.

It's normal for a horse to scratch itself sometimes, as this foal is doing. But continual scratching might mean the horse has a skin disease.

Common complaints

The illnesses below are common, and not easy to prevent. If someone thinks that their horse may have any of them, they need to call a vet.

A **persistent cough** can be caused by an infection or a dust allergy.

Inflamed and cracked hooves are a symptom of **mud fever**. This is usually caused by standing in wet, muddy ground.

Colic gives a horse a stomach ache, and makes it restless and sweaty. The horse might kick itself, paw the ground or roll around.

If a horse has **laminitis**, its feet swell and heat up. It is caused by wearing ill-fitting shoes or eating too much rich grass.

Here are some more signs to look out for that may mean a horse is unwell:

U Runny nose
U Cold, drooping ears
U Coat standing on end
U Dry skin
U Limping
U Loss of appetite

Coughing is a sign that something is wrong with a horse's lungs or air passages.

Horses sometimes roll like this to groom themselves, but a horse that's rolling violently may be trying to relieve the pain of colic.

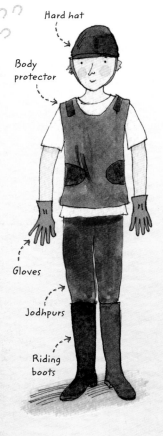

In ancient Greece, jockeys competing in horse races rode completely naked.

Hard hat

Body protector

Gloves

Jodhpurs

Riding boots

Clothing

Riding a horse can be a rough and dangerous business, so riders need clothes that will protect them and last a long time. Sometimes even the horses need to put on a few protective layers too.

Riding gear

What riders wear has to be flexible enough to let them move freely, but also tough enough to withstand the constant motion that riding involves. The best riding clothes are both comfortable and hard-wearing.

Riders never mount a horse without a **hard hat**. It protects their head from damage if they fall or a horse kicks them.

Riding boots are sturdy, with strong toes to help protect the rider's feet if the horse steps on them. They have small heels to stop the rider's feet from sliding through the stirrups.

Jodhpurs are tight-fitting riding trousers made of tough, stretchy material. They're often reinforced at the knees and can be tucked into longer riding boots or worn over shorter boots.

54

Horse clothes

Usually, a horse's natural coat is enough to keep it safe and warm. But, in the winter months, or if it's ill or travelling in a horsebox, a horse might need clothing. Warm, waterproof hoods and rugs protect a horse's head and body from cold and rain. Protective boots and caps, usually made from leather and felt, keep the horse from injuring itself while travelling.

Poll guard

Travel boots

This horse is wearing a rug and hood to keep it warm during a cold winter night in its paddock.

Horse power

Throughout history, horses and ponies have been used for travel, and to pull vehicles and machinery. Until cars and trains took over around 150 years ago, the only way to travel quickly or move heavy loads was by horse.

Chariots and carts

From the Bronze Age right up to the 19th century, the fastest way to get around was by horse-drawn chariot, cart or carriage.

Chariots were light, open vehicles with two or four wheels. They were pulled by at least two horses running side by side. A chariot had standing room only, for no more than two people. It was used for transport, for hunting, in battles, and in races.

In a cart, the driver sits at the front, and carries goods or extra people in the back. Carts usually have two wheels. Those that have four wheels are known as coaches or carriages.

In ancient China, when a rich and powerful man died, his horse-drawn chariot, its driver and two of his horses were sealed into the tomb with his body.

Chariot racing was extremely popular in ancient Rome. One writer of the time said that Roman people only needed bread and chariot races.

Cross-country travel

In the 19th century, thousands of people journeyed across America, looking for land on which to settle. They travelled in covered wagons, which they called prairie schooners. Horses had to pull whole families, as well as all their belongings, in journeys lasting up to six months, over rough and dangerous territory.

A prairie schooner could take a load of 1½ tonnes, though the lighter the wagon, the less the chances of it getting stuck in muddy ground.

Pulling together

If you travelled back in time just 100 years anywhere in the world, you'd find horses hard at work. They were tough and powerful animals that pulled heavy loads, such as ploughs on farms, barges along canals, fire engines on roads, trucks of coal down mines, and even cannons on battlefields.

In some countries, horses, like this Polish draught horse, are still used for pulling heavy farm equipment.

If you want to travel up some of the world's steepest mountains, you may need ponies to carry your luggage for you. Mountain ponies can pick their way over rocky trails that are too dangerous for even the most reliable off-road vehicles.

Horses at work

Over the last hundred years, most working horses have been replaced by machinery. Tractors, buses, barges and trucks that once used horse power are now powered by engines instead. But there are still some places where you can see horses hard at work, putting their grace, reliability and intelligence to good use.

On the farm

All across the world, livestock, such as sheep and cattle, are looked after by ranchers and farm hands on horseback. The workers move herds safely from place to place, making sure none get left behind. In some places, farm workers now do this on quad bikes instead, but horses are better suited to the task where the ground is steep or rocky. Also, livestock that are easily startled tend to respond better to horses, as they are much quieter than quad bikes.

Cattle horses have to be calm and patient around young or nervous livestock.

Police work

Horses are used by police forces to patrol remote areas that can't easily be reached by car. They're also used to control crowds during large gatherings, such as sports events and protest marches. Mounted police can see out over the crowd to direct its movement and pick out any trouble-makers.

These police horses are being trained to be at ease in their protective riot gear and to cope with situations where their vision is limited.

On parade

Even though horses are rarely used in warfare any more, many military forces around the world have mounted divisions that perform in military parades. The horses and their riders dress in highly decorated ceremonial uniforms, and take part in processions and perform military displays.

In British military parades, big, strong horses carry drummers playing heavy drums.

How to draw horses

If you like horses, you might enjoy drawing them. They can be tricky to draw, but this simple pencil and paint technique shows you how to sketch a horse by looking at its body as a series of shapes and lines. By following these steps, you can draw a galloping horse, and pick up some useful tips on how to show movement.

To get the shape of a horse's legs right, look at a picture of a horse in the position you want. Copy the shape of its legs by drawing zigzags as a guide.

This drawing of a horse shows you how its body is made up of shapes and lines.

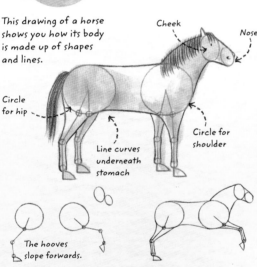

Cheek

Nose

Circle for hip

Line curves underneath stomach

Circle for shoulder

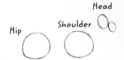

Hip

Shoulder

Head

1. With a pencil, lightly draw two circles for a shoulder and hip. Draw two ovals for a head, making the nose smaller than the cheek.

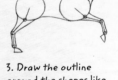

The hooves slope forwards.

2. Draw zigzag legs from the middle of the shoulder and the hip. Add small circles for the joints. Then add triangles with curved tops for the hooves.

3. Draw the outline around the shapes like this, arching the neck. When you have finished, erase the lines from inside the horse's body.

Bump for other nostril

4. Add an ear pointing backwards, to show that the horse is running. Erase the top part of the head that overlaps the ear. Add an eye and nostrils.

5. Draw two more zigzags for the other legs. Add hooves. Then, draw the legs around the zigzags and erase the lines inside the legs.

6. For a mane and tail, draw long lines streaming out from the horse's rear and neck. This makes it look like the horse is moving quickly.

Paint in the mane and tail.

7. Mix some coloured ink or paint with water to make a pale shade. Paint the parts of the body shaded here to show the horse's shape.

8. When the paint is dry, draw over the outline with a pencil of the same colour. You can vary the pressure on the pencil to get thick and thin lines.

You can flick paint from a paintbrush around the horse's feet to make it look like it's galloping through mud, earth or water.

There are around 58 million horses in the world. Here are the top ten countries with the highest horse populations:

U USA
U China
U Mexico
U Brazil
U Argentina
U Colombia
U Mongolia
U Ethiopia
U Russia
U Kazakhstan

Amazing but true

Here are some intriguing and extraordinary facts that you may not know about horses.

Tall and small

Often over 17 hands high – 172cm (5½ft) tall – Shirehorses are the tallest breed of horse. They are the star attractions of agricultural shows and military parades in Britain.

Fallabellas are the world's smallest horses. Their maximum height is just 7 hands high – 72cm (28in) – which is about the size of a big dog. They can only be ridden by very little children.

A fully grown Fallabella is just over knee-high to a Shirehorse.

Through the nose

Horses can only breathe through their noses and not through their mouths. That's why you'll never see a horse panting.

This horse is galloping hard, so is flaring its nostrils wide to take in as much air as it can.

On guard

It's very unusual to see a group of horses in the same field all lying down at once. This is because one animal always stands on the look-out for danger.

The oldest horse on record was "Old Billy," an English draught horse, that lived to be 62. Horses usually live until they're in their mid 20s.

Bone-less

Arab horses have short backs for their size. This is because they have one fewer ribs, back bones and neck bones than all other types of horse.

Sleep tight

Horses often sleep standing up. In the wild, sleeping on their feet means that they can make a quick getaway if a predator attacks.

Horses "lock" the muscles in their lower legs so they can fall asleep without falling over.

63

INDEX

behaviour 12, 14-15, 16, 17, 36
breeds 8-9
  Andalusians 9
  Arabs 8, 63
  Fallabellas 62
  Hackneys 9
  Lipizzaners 39
  Przewalskis 9
  Shirehorses 9, 62
  Thoroughbreds 8
  Welsh mountain ponies 9
brushing 37, 48-49
carts 34, 56
classical riding 22-23, 24, 42
cleaning 45, 48-49, 50, 51
coat colours 10-11
colts 12
communication 14-15, 16-17
cross-country events 23, 30, 31
dressage 24-25, 30
eventing see horse trials
farms 8, 57, 58
farriers 50, 51
feeding 44, 46-47
fillies 12

foals 12-13, 14, 18, 20, 48, 52, 61
gaits 18-19, 21, 24, 36
  canter 19, 24, 38, 43
  flying pace 19
  gallop 19, 39
  pace 34
  trot 18, 24, 25, 34
  walk 18, 24, 42, 43
gymkhanas 23, 28-29
hacking 43
halt 19
hands (measurement) 7, 62
history 6, 22, 23, 28, 30, 32, 38, 40, 54, 56-57
horseball 35
horseboxes 32, 55
horse shows 8, 36-37
horse trials 30-31
jumps 26, 27, 30, 31, 34
mares 12
markings 11, 60
mounted games 23, 28, 29, 40, 41
paces see gaits
paddocks 46, 47, 48, 55
parades 23, 59, 62
points 7

polo 35
racing 28, 29, 31, 32-33, 34, 50
  flat 32, 33
  harness 34
  hurdle 34
  road and track 31
  steeplechase 31, 32
  trotting 34
riding equipment 20, 22, 23, 40
rodeos 23, 40-41
show jumping 23, 26-27, 30
stables 8, 32, 43, 44-45, 46, 47, 49
stallions 12, 14
stunts 39
trail riding 23, 42
training 20-21
trekking 42
types of horse 8-9
  draught 8, 9, 63
  harness 9
  riding 9, 50
vets 31, 52, 53
Western riding 22-23, 42
wild horses 14, 17, 46, 48, 51, 63

PHOTO CREDITS